Adobe
Firefly
Unleashed:
The Ultimate Guide

Adobe
Firefly
Unleashed:
The Ultimate Guide

Unlock the Full Potential of Adobe Firefly;
Learn Essential Techniques, Tips and
Tricks for Designing Stunning Visuals
and Interactive Experiences

Eric Edward

CONTENTS

CHAPTER 1

Introduction to Adobe Photoshop

The Adobe Photoshop is a powerful design software which has an abundance of tools to choose from, and this might be confusing to use at first glance. You should note however that Photoshop and its features were not designed for professionals only. With practice, you can easily teach yourself to create and design beautifully compelling graphics. All that is needed is a good understanding of its core elements, and you too can become a professional designer.

Specifications and System Requirements for Installing Adobe Photoshop

Your device must pass certain requirement before you can install the Photoshop software on it. If it cannot meet the requirements, then you would have to purchase a new PC before you can enjoy the new features that comes with the Adobe Photoshop. The table below shows the requirements needed for a computer to operate with the Photoshop software successfully.

Windows

	Minimum	Recommended
Processor	2 GHz or faster multicore Intel or AMD processor with 64-bit capability and SSE 4.2 or later	
Operating System	Preferably Windows 10 64-bit (version 20H2); Versions of LTSC are not supported.	
RAM	8 GB	16 GB or more

Graphics Card	• DirectX 12 (feature level 12_0 or later)-capable GPU • GPUs with 1.5 GB of memory; • GPUs that are under 7 years old. We do not currently support testing on GPUs older than seven years.	• GPU that supports DirectX 12 at feature level 12_0 or above. • 4 GB of GPU memory or more for 4K displays
	Visit the Photoshop graphics card FAQ for further information.	
Monitor Resolution	Displaying at 100% UI scaling in 1280 by 800	minimum 1920 x 1080 display at 100% UI scaling
Hard Disk space	20 GB of free hard drive space	50 GB of free hard disk space A quick internal SSD for installing apps; A different internal drive for scratch drives.

Internet	Software activation, subscription verification, and access to online services all require an internet connection and registration.	
	Minimum	**Recommended**
Processor	ARM processor	
Operating system	Windows 10 64-bit (version 20H2) or later on a Windows 10 ARM device	
RAM	8 GB	16 GB or more
Graphics Card	GPU memory of 4 GB	

The rest of ARM's features are identical to those of Intel.

Mac OS

	Minimum	Recommended
Processor	2 GHz or faster multicore Intel® CPU with SSE 4.2 or later and 64-bit support	
Operating system	Mac OS Big Sur (11.0) or a later version	Big Sur (version 11) of Mac OS V10.15.x installations are prohibited.
RAM	8 GB	16 GB or more
Graphics Card	• Metal-supporting GPU • A GPU with 1.5 GB of RAM	• Metal-supporting GPU • 4 GB of GPU memory or more for 4K displays
	Check out Mac machines that support Metal to determine whether your device is compatible. Visit the Photoshop graphics card FAQ for further information.	
Monitor Resolution	Displaying at 100% UI scaling in 1280 by 800	minimum 1920 x 1080 display at 100% UI scaling

Hard Disk Space	20 GB of free hard drive space	50 GB of free hard drive space quick internal SSD for installing apps Extra fast drive(s) or SSD to create scratch disks
	Installing Photoshop will not work on a drive with a case-sensitive file system.	
Internet	Software activation, membership verification, and access to online services all require an internet connection and registration.	

	Minimum	Recommended
Processor	Apple Silicon processor built on ARM	
Operating system	later than Mac OS Big Sur (version 11.2.2)	
RAM	8 GB	16 GB or more

The rest of Apple Silicon's features are same to those of Intel.

Overview of the Photoshop interface

Due to the fact Photoshop is designed majorly for professional use, the user interface might feel a tad too complex and overwhelming for new or casual users. that is why it is most important, that you get familiarized with the main elements on the Photoshop interface. Photoshop is a tool that can be used for practically any form of image manipulation, from enhancing images to producing graphics of the highest caliber. The Photoshop user interface consists of;

➤ Opening Files.

➤ Working with panels and the toolbar.

➤ Customizing the workspace.

➤ Changing the display size.

Opening files

Instead of producing a new image from scratch, you can opt to open an existing one. Existing image files, such as JPEG, PNG, and PSD (Photoshop document) files, can be opened and edited with Photoshop.

To open a file;

i. Choose File > Open. Browse through and locate the file you wish to open, then select it.

ii. Click the Open drop-down (above the tool box). The Open drop-down is a list of recently opened files.

iii. Drag an image from a folder on your computer or storage device, and drop it in the Editor. The file will appear in Photoshop.

Working with Panels and the Toolbar

As earlier stated, Photoshop comes along with a very wide array of tools to choose from, and this could make working with it a bit daunting, as it might be difficult to grasp such a huge number of functions at once. Prepared below is a clear and concise guide to main Photoshop tool bar, their functions and where they can be located. To make it easier, the tools have been grouped into categories where they belong.

1. Selection Tools

The Selection Tool allows you to select different portions of an image that you wish to edit. Each of these tools has its own specific functions.

► **Lasso Tool:** It is used for free outlining around an object. This tools allows for freehand selections, and is best employed for areas that do not qualify as shapes.

► **Quick Selection Tool:** This offers to select and deselect in Photoshop an object quickly and hassle-free using just one brush. This tool works best on an area with clearly defined edges.

► **Rectangular Marquee Tool:** This is used for outlining rectangular selections.

► **Elliptical Marquee Tool:** This is used for outlining elliptical selections.

► **Magic Wand Tool:** In Photoshop finds the parts of the image with the same color as the one you have chosen and selects them. You can decide to set Tolerance in the Options palette of the Magic Wand tool. The higher the value, the more colors will fall in a selected area.

Other Selection Tools include:

► **Move Tool:** The move tool is designed for moving layers, selections, and guides in your project.

► **Single Row Marquee Tool:** It is employed when we need to pick one row of pixels on the canvas from left to right.

► **Single Column Marquee Tool:** It is employed when we need to pick one row of pixels on the canvas from top to bottom.

► **Polygonal Lasso Tool:** This is used for polygonal outlining of an object with straight edges.

► **Magnetic Lasso Tool:** This selects an object in such a way that its outline is bound to the object's edges while moving the cursor.

2. Crop and Slice Tools

You may also use the Crop and Slice category features in the Photoshop toolbar for splitting your project into separate components for subsequent extraction and use.

► **Crop Tool:** The crop tool is used to crop images and remove unnecessary details from them. The only difference separating it and the Rectangular Marquee tool is that when you press the "Enter" key, your image gets cropped to correspond with the size of the box.

► **Perspective Crop Tool:** For resizing your canvas and correcting distortion and perspective difficulties, apply the Perspective Crop Tool.

➤ **The Slice Tool:** Using this tool, you can split a document or even a layout into portions of different dimensions. You can use it to split up an image into multiple.

3. Measuring Tools

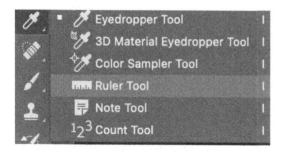

The measurement tools featured in the Photoshop toolbar enables you to choose a color from an image's layers and save a set of color values for use later.

With the tools in this area, you can measure items, align an image, as well as add notes.

4. Eyedropper Tool

This tool renders a sample of colors from your project. It allows for you to recreate a hue from a website or current project. It is used to obtain a color from a picture for future use.

How to Use the Eyedropper Tool

Select the icon from the sidebar. Next, locate that color you would like to extract, and simply click that area to clone the color.

Once you've extracted the color, you'll see it indicated both in the Color module at the top right of your screen, as well as the bottom of the left sidebar. You can double-click that color box to bring up the advanced color picker, where you can then adjust and save the color to a swatch for future use.

▶ **3D Material Eyedropper Tool:** It provides sample content derived from a 3D model.

▶ **Color Sampler Tool:** This tool can be used to match colors in an image but its values can be stored in the Info palette for future reference. Users can sample max 4 parts at once. If you want to study color data, refer to the Info panel.

► **Ruler Tool:** It is employed to calculate angles, locations, and lengths. The Ruler tool determines the amount of space between any two workspace points. It is excellent for arranging tasks and items precisely the way you need to.

► **Note Tool:** This is good for including text messages as attachments to your project. The PSD document is saved with them in PS. The notes could be written down or recorded as audio.

► **Count Tool:** This enables you to manually add up all the items in the image. Otherwise, the application enables automatic part-counting for the given image.

5. Type Tools

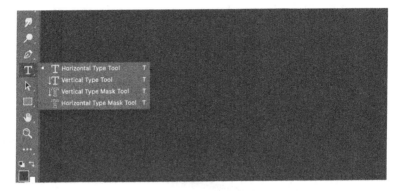

The Type tools allows you to add texts and edit corresponding parameters (such as size, font, etc.), Knowledge of its capabilities is essential, especially if you want to add titles to the designs you create.

▶ **Horizontal Type Tool:** The function of this tool is to enable you to add texts to your project horizontally, i.e. left to right. It performs horizontal type adding to the project.

▶ **Vertical Type Tool:** You can add texts to the project utilizing the Vertical Type Tool, but it does so vertically, from the top to the bottom.

▶ **Vertical Type Mask Tool:** Instead of just adding the editable text, the Vertical Type

Mask Tool vertically outlines the type shape.

➤ **Horizontal Type Mask Tool:** The same functions as the aforementioned tool are also performed by the horizontal type mask tool.

6. Navigation Tools

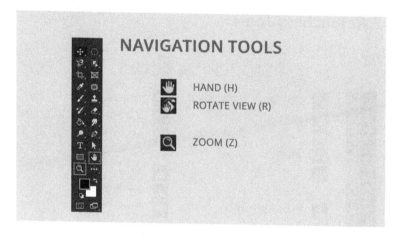

You may move your project around, zoom in on an image, flip the workspace, and do a lot more with the help of the Navigation Toolbar.

➤ **Hand Tool:** You can move your project across the screen with the hand tool. This is crucial, especially if you want to zoom in on a certain area of a photo to see the results more clearly.

▶ **Rotate View Tool:** With this tool, you can rotate your project to view and edit it from any angle.

▶ **Zoom Tool:** You can zoom in on your image using the zoom tool, as the name suggests.

7. Retouching Tools

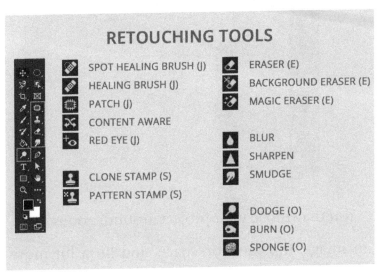

The Retouching Tools area provides tools to fix broken images, apply recurring patterns, change an image's colors, and many other options.

▶ **The Spot Healing Brush Tool** is used to fix and erase blemishes, undesirable stains, and damaged areas of your image.

► **Healing Brush Tool:** Using this tool, you can paint over larger flaws to make them disappear.

► **Patch Tool:** With the help of pixels from another region or a pattern, a specified area can be repaired with this tool. This is accomplished by drawing a freehand outline around the area of the image that contains the desired defections.

► **Red Eye Tool:** This is mostly used to fix widespread red-eye issues brought on by camera flashes.

► **The Clone Stamp Tool** is used to duplicate objects, remove tattoos, correct imperfections on a model's face, and clean dust from an image. The Rubber Stamp Tool is yet another name for it.

► **The Pattern Stamp Tool** is available for adding any pattern to the image.

➤ **Eraser Tool:** This tool is excellent for erasing pixels within a layer and is used to swiftly delete errant pixels or isolated shapes from an image. By overpainting them, the Background Eraser Tool makes it easier to remove canvas elements of the same hue.

➤ **Magic Eraser Tool:** This tool allows you to quickly locate and pick canvas elements of the same color for deletion with just one click.

➤ **Blur Tool:** This tool enables painting over areas that have been further softened and blurred.

➤ **Sharpen Tool:** This tool provides the same functionality as the one listed before, but sharpens rather than blurs.

➤ **The Smudge Tool:** This tool is intended to simulate finger painting.

➤ **Dodge Tool:** This tool enables you to lighten previously overpainted areas.

> **Burn Tool:** This tool provides the same functionality as the one before, but with a darker effect rather than a lighter one.

> **The Sponge Tool** alludes to saturation and suggests a rise or reduction in it.

8. Painting Tools

Photoshop's painting tools are made to alter images with brushstrokes and coloring to simulate drawing on a canvas.

> **Brush Tool:** A basic drawing tool is the brush tool. It is used to paint any image, starting with a chosen size and color. Additionally, it is

utilized on layer masks to reveal or conceal portions of the image.

- **The Pencil Tool** is still another fundamental drawing tool; however, it only allows for the creation of hard-edged lines.

- **Color Replacement Tool:** This tool lets you alter the hue, brightness, saturation, and color values.

- **The Mixer Brush Tool** is ideal for imitating actual painting. It may provide effects like wet paint, color blending, and more.

- **History Brush Tool:** This tool functions similarly to the Brush Tool, with the exception that the data it uses to paint with comes from the image's initial state.

- **Art historical Brush Tool:** This tool allows you to use a historical state to apply paint styles to your image.

- **Gradient Tool:** With this tool, you may create color gradients by simply drawing a seamless transition between two colors.

- ➤ **Paint Bucket Tool:** This tool enables you to add a pattern or the Foreground color to an area of a picture that is the same color. In the zone you select in the Tolerance parameter, you can determine which hues and colors that are comparable will be handled.

- ➤ **The 3D Material Drop Tool** is excellent for taking material samples from one area of a picture and subsequently dropping them into different areas of the model, mesh, or 3D layer.

9. Drawing Tools

The Photoshop drawing tools are intended for the creation and modification of vector objects. These tools perform effectively when used with vector-based paths, which frequently become selections.

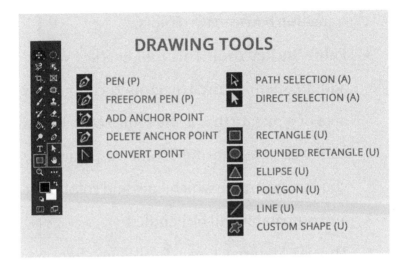

► **The Pen Tool** is a tool for drawing paths. Every time we need to draw a distinct vector route, shape, or selection, it is useful.

► **Freeform Pen Tool:** Using this tool, we can draw matrix shapes and paths (shape outlines) just like we would if we were sketching with a pencil on paper. While drawing, the tool automatically adds anchor points.

► **Add Anchor Point Tool:** This tool expands the path's number of points of reference.

► **The Delete Anchor Point Tool** removes any existing reference points from the path.

➤ **Convert Point Tool:** With this tool, we can alter a path point as well as examine the tangle of lines and points that we have drawn with the other pen tools.

➤ **Path Selection Tool:** Using anchor points, direction lines, and direction points, the path selection tool selects a shape or segment.

➤ **Direct Selection Tool:** With this tool, a distinct section of the path, reference point, or direction guide is selected and moved.

➤ **Rectangle Tool:** This tool is excellent for creating rectangle paths, pixels, or vector-based shapes. You can give it rounded and pointed corners.

➤ **Ellipse Tool:** This tool is used to create pixel or vector-based elliptical shapes.

➤ **Triangle Tool:** This tool provides the same functionality as the previous one but in the form of a triangle.

▶ **The Polygon Tool** facilitates the creation of polygonal shapes. Create as many sides as necessary.

▶ **Line Tool:** You can create precisely straight lines and even arrows using this tool.

▶ **Custom Shape Tool:** This tool enables you to choose and create a unique shape.

Setting Up the Toolbar

You can alter the Toolbar to make navigating simpler and to make Photoshop as comfortable for you as feasible. You might design a workspace that best suits your needs and brings out the best in your creative ability by customizing the toolbar.

Moving the Toolbar

Drag and drop operations predominate in the Customize Toolbar dialog. The toolbar is immediately updated if a tool is removed or moved. Locate the vertical line symbol at the toolbar's top and

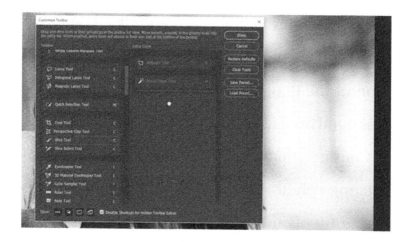

drag it to the desired location to change the position of the Photoshop toolbar. The panel will be unbound from its default position as a result.

Including a New Column

By dragging a tool out of its nested location and dropping it between two sections, you can even make your own brand-new sets of nested tools. To construct your own unique new set, you can then drag & drop other tools under that new section.

Drag and drop operations predominate in the Customize Toolbar dialog. The toolbar is immediately updated if a tool is removed or moved. Locate the vertical line symbol at the toolbar's top and drag it to the desired location to change the position of the Photoshop toolbar. The panel will be unbound from its default position as a result.

Consider that you are creating a new brand, altering a photo, or working in 3D. You might have a set of tools that you use frequently for each of these duties. Finding the specific tools every time, you need them with the default toolbar is rather annoying. The answer is to design a special toolbar that launches as soon as you select the correct workspace.

The relevant Photoshop panels will appear when you select the desired work type from the Workspaces dropdown box. Then you can rearrange everything, opening the tools you typically use and closing the ones you don't.

You will have access to your personalized toolbars each time you open the Workspace. To make things simpler to remember, you can even give each tool a unique set of keyboard shortcuts.

Drag the workspace to New Workspace to bring up the Save New Workspace window and save the customized workspace and toolbars. Give the new workspace a name, confirm the keyboard shortcuts, menus, and toolbars, then click Save.

CHAPTER 2

Saving Images

In Photoshop, saving your work works a little differently than it does in other programs. Unlike Microsoft Word, which only supports one primary file format (.docx), Photoshop provides a number of options to store your photographs.

Optional Savings

You can choose from a number of options and file types when saving a file in Photoshop:

PSD: Although you do not have to use it for every image, it is the standard file type for Photoshop documents. PSD will save all of the information about your image, including its layers, allowing you to edit it again at a later time. Since PSD files are made to be opened in Photoshop, you will also need to save a copy of the image in a widely used file format, such as JPEG, if you wish to share it with others.

Common file types: JPEG and PNG are only two examples of the basic file types in which you can save photographs. These file formats are ideal for sharing with others since they can be viewed and altered on practically any computer or mobile device. These formats cannot store layer information, making them less helpful than PSD files if you intend to keep modifying the file.

Save for Web: You should utilize the Save for Web tool if you intend to upload an image to the Web, such as on a blog or website. You can use this application to save web-optimized photos, which will make them simpler to download and view online.

The option to resize images is one of the many helpful options included in Save for Web for optimizing images for the Web.

The saving method you select will ultimately rely on what you need to do with the image.

Using Save As

PSD files can be saved in addition to other popular formats like JPEG and PNG using the Save As command.

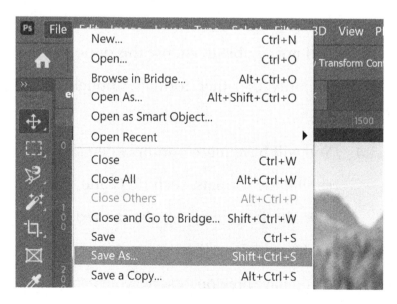

1. In Photoshop, open the image and choose File > Save As.

2. There will be a dialog box. After choosing a location, type the appropriate file name. To prevent mistakenly overwriting the original file, you should create a new file with a different name.

3. Select the required file format by clicking the Format menu. We will save this picture as a JPEG file for our example. Make sure Layers is selected if you are saving as a PSD file. You will not be able to choose this option in the majority of other formats, though. Press Save.

4. You will have more options when saving in several file formats, such JPEG and TIFF. To save the image, choose the desired quality setting and then click OK.

5. If you have previously saved your project as a PSD file, you can always save your progress

by choosing File > Save or by using Ctrl+S (or Command+S on a Mac). To prevent over-writing your original file when dealing with another format, such as JPEG, we advise using Save As.

Sometimes when saving a file, you might not have selected every available format. You must choose the Enable legacy "Save as" checkbox. To enable Legacy "Save as," select File Handling > Edit > Preferences > Ctrl + K, and then click OK.

Save For Web

You must choose a few options for the image you are saving when you utilize the Save for Web tool.

File format: You can select one of a few Web-safe file formats when using Save for Web. For images, you will typically utilize the JPEG format. When compared to PNG-8, which is typically used for graphics and illustrations with limited colors,

PNG-24 will maintain the entire quality of the image. The GIF and WBMP formats are typically not necessary.

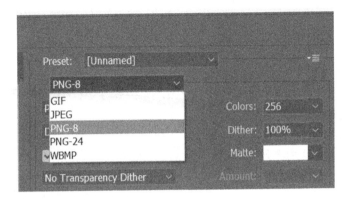

Image size: From the Save for Web dialog box, you can resize the image. The file size will be decreased by downsizing the image. However, you probably will not need to resize your photographs if you are using a service like Facebook or Tumblr

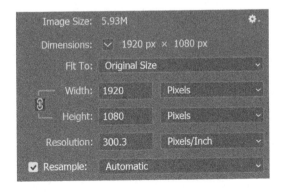

because these platforms do it for you.

Quality: If you are using the JPEG format, you can save the image at several degrees of quality. To get the ideal balance between quality and file size, you might wish to try out various options.

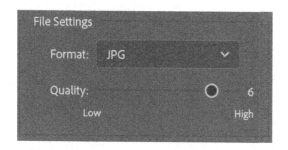

Procedures for "Save for Web"

1. Go to File > Save for Web.

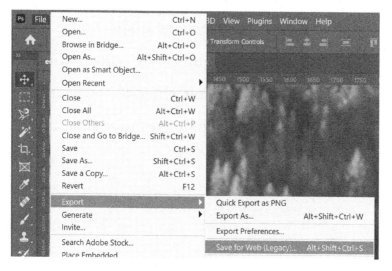

2. The Save for Web dialog box will show up.
    Choose the file type and quality setting that
    you want.

3. Resize the image if necessary by entering the
    required measurements under Image Size.
    The height ought to be automatically
    adjusted when you enter the new image
    width in order to preserve the original aspect
    ratio.

4. If you would like, you may compare the original image with a preview of the updated version using the 2-Up view. This is a simple approach to make sure you have not sacrificed too much of the original version's quality. Each preview window's lower-left corner displays the file size.

5. Press Save. An additional dialog box will open. Click Save after entering the desired file name and location for the file. To prevent mistakenly overwriting the original file, you

should create a new file with a different
name.

CHAPTER 3

Understanding Layers

Do you ever ponder how other designers use Photoshop to get such fantastic results? Their proficiency with the Layers tool is the key to their success. One of the most crucial things to understand when beginning to edit in Photoshop is layers. It is unquestionably one of Photoshop's best features. Professionals frequently use Layers in most of their projects, if not all of them. Probably the most crucial thing you can do to advance your Photoshop abilities is to learn how to use layers.

What Are Layers?

Different photos are stacked on top of one another to form layers. Imagine layers as transparent glass pane sheets piled on top of one another. This enables you to make alterations to an image without changing the original image data, i.e., you can use each layer independently of the others to do so. On one layer, elements can be drawn, edited, pasted, and repositioned without affecting the others. Each layer in the image remains separate from the rest until you join, or merge, the layers. They combine to create the final image. Using layers has the benefit of allowing you to save your project in Photoshop with all of your layers intact. The use of layers for non-destructive editing is thus possible.

Your Photoshop edits will not obliterate the source picture. All the additional data and images you want to include in the original file are contained in the layers. Layers can be used to add text, combine images, change colors, add vector shapes, and even add special effects. A trendy image or any other type of graphical work requires layers. Working with every element of an image simultaneously without impacting other elements of the image is difficult. In these situations, layers give us a flexible approach to add or change a particular portion of the image and combine it with other portions of the image. Amazing ways to control an image are possible using layers. Getting used to the layers will take some time.

Layer Panel

The first layer you see when you open a picture will always be called "Background Layer." You are free to add as many additional layers as you like on top of this one. In the Layers panel, you can see every added layer.

Although you can order them as you choose, naming them is more crucial. By naming the layers, you may avoid getting lost and navigate and identify them more easily than if they all have the same name.

The Layer Panel's Parts

1. **Layer Group:** By putting layers into a folder, layers can be grouped. A folder with numerous layers is called a layer group.

2. **Type Layer:** Similar to the text layer, the Type layer can be modified. Similar to the Image layer, it is.

3. **Adaptation Layer:** Adjustment Layers are layers that have certain adjustments applied to them, such as changing the colors or tones of all the levels below them. Only the layers beneath it will be impacted, while other layers are left unaffected.

4. **Layer Style:** The Layer style is an effect-containing layer. To switch the layer style on or off, click the eye icon. When a layer is

double-clicked, the layer's style options are displayed. Layer styles comprise of:

➤ **Opacity** - Modify the layer's opacity.

➤ **Stroke** - Draw a layer's outline.

➤ **Inner Shadow** - Creates a shadow inside the layer to create the impression that it is entering.

➤ **Inner radiance** - Create an internal radiance.

➤ Add a color as an overlay to the layer.

➤ **Gradient Overlay** - Overlay the layer with a gradient.

➤ **Overlay with a pattern** - Place a pattern on top of the layer.

➤ Put an outside glow around the layer.

➤ **Drop Shadow** - Add a shadow to the layer's base to give the appearance that it is floating.

5. **Layer Mask:** For non-destructive editing, a layer's layer mask is crucial. The visual com-

ponents are seen and hidden by painting on the mask.

6. **Smart Object:** A smart object is a particular layer or container that may hold various types of items, including layers, vectors, videos, raw files, 3D models, etc.

7. **Background Layer:** Every image has a background layer by default, which is located in front of the image's content. Because it is locked by default and must be unlocked in order to be worked on, it is often referred to as the unseen layer. An image's background can be changed or made translucent using the background layer. We can also select a translucent background when producing a picture, which will add a transparent background layer.

Adding Layers

The Layers panel is located on the right, but if for some reason it isn't, you may bring it up by choosing Layers from the Window menu.

Remove Layers

The method of deleting a layer is as simple as creating a new layer. To delete a layer, either select the delete option from the context menu when you right-click on it or go to the layer panel and look for the delete icon near the bottom of the panel.

The option to delete the layer will be presented; select Yes to proceed.

The Delete key can also be used to confirm deletion. It will not request confirmation. By pressing the shift key while clicking on a layer, we can select many layers at once.

You can undo operations at any moment by pressing the Ctrl + Alt + Z buttons.

Managing Layers

Multiple layer adjustments are possible in Photoshop. Effective layer stack management is possible. On layers, we can carry out a number of actions, including move, transform, reorder, group, etc.

Rearranging Layers

A layer can be moved up or down by clicking on it and dragging it.

Show the Layer Panel

Use the f7 key or the Window-> Layer menu to bring up the Photoshop Layer Panel.

Duplicate Layers

To make several tweaks without impacting the original layer, we can duplicate a layer.

Right-click the layer and choose "Duplicate Layer" to make a copy of it.

When prompted for approval, select Yes to duplicate the layer.

The layer will be duplicated with the same content.

How to Create a Layer Group

A layer group is an assembly of various layers. Groups are helpful for project organization since they keep the layer's panel clean.

Any of the following procedures can be used to build a layer group:

1. From the layer panel's options, choose New Group to create a new layer group. Drag and drop layers into the newly created layer group.

2. Select the New Group from Layers option in the layers panel options after selecting all the layers that we want to group. All the chosen layers will be added to a group that is created by the program.

3. Alternatively, you can move the layers inside the folder icon provided at the bottom of the layer panels by using Windows' Alt-drag or Mac OS' Option-drag commands on the layers. It will prompt you to confirm the

process and establish a new group.

Ungrouping Layers

Right-click the layer group and choose Ungroup Layers to remove all of the layers from it. The group will be deleted along with all of the levels that were grouped.

Linking Layers

Two or more levels or groups can be linked. Layers are linked together to form a relationship, which they will maintain until we unlink them. To linked layers, we can apply or move transformation.

Select the layers or groups you want to link, then click the link icon at the bottom of the layer panel.

Select the layers or groups you want to unlink, then click the link button once again. It will remove the layer links.

The connected layers can be temporarily disabled. Temporarily shift-click the link symbol to unlink them, then repeat the process to relink them.

Showing and Hiding Layers

Click the eye icon next to the selected layers to make a layer invisible. Click on this symbol once more to reveal the layer.

CHAPTER 4

Accessing the Photoshop Preferences

To gain access the Preferences, on a PC, go up to the Edit menu in the Menu Bar along the top of the screen. From there, choose Preferences from the pop up options provided, and then General.

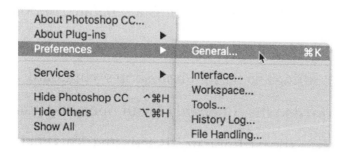

The Preference dialog box would then appear as a result of this. The categories that are available are shown in the column on the left. The primary area in the center displays options for the category that is now selected.

Export Clipboard

The Export Clipboard option is the first to investigate in the General Preferences. Your computer's overall performance may be impacted by this choice. The copied elements are added to Photoshop's clipboard when we copy and paste pictures or layers. The portion of your computer's memory (RAM) designated for Photoshop use is the clipboard, so to speak. The operating system of your computer also contains a separate clipboard (a separate chunk of memory).

All things kept in Photoshop's clipboard are exported to the clipboard of your operating system when "Export Clipboard" is activated. This enables you to copy the content and then paste it into another program, such as Adobe Illustrator or InDesign. However, because Photoshop files are frequently very large, exporting them into your operating system's RAM may be difficult and might result in errors and performance issues.

"Export Clipboard" is enabled by default. Choose not to use this option or turn it off to keep your computer operating efficiently. It is advisable to simply save the file in Photoshop rather than transferring it from Photoshop to another app. Next, launch the other software and open the saved file:

, Grid & Slices

ns

☐ Beep When Done
☑ Dynamic Color Sliders
☐ Export Clipboard
☑ Use Shift Key for Tool Switch
☑ Resize Image During Place

Interface Preferences

Let us now have a look at a few settings that allow us to modify Photoshop's user interface. On the left, select the Interface category.

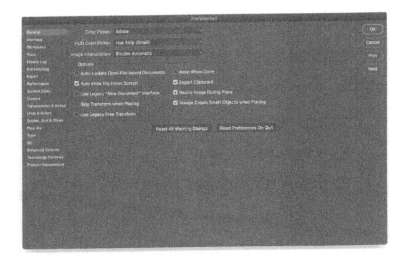

1. Color Palette

The general color of Photoshop's user interface is managed by this color theme setting. In this context, "color" simply refers to various grayscale tones. Adobe offers us a selection of four alternative color schemes. A swatch is used to represent each theme. The second swatch from the left is the default color scheme. Click on the swatch of the other color scheme if you decide to use it. The appearance of the user interface is the only difference between themes, some of which are lighter than others. Select the subject matter that most appeals to you. The Preferences section in Photoshop allows you to alter the color scheme at any moment.

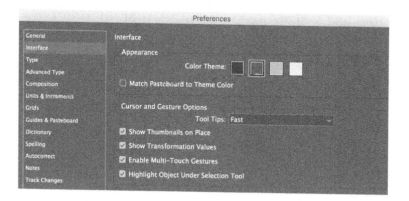

2. UI Font Size

This setting regulates the font size used in Photoshop's user interface. Photoshop's default text size is tiny. You can always increase the size, though, if you have difficulties reading the small type or prefer a larger font. Choose either the

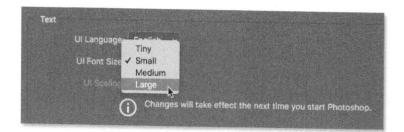

medium or large option to enlarge the text. You can reduce the text size if you like a much smaller font size, though. Choose the smallest option to reduce the text's size. Keep in mind that in order for changes to take effect, Photoshop must be closed and restarted.

Tools Preferences

1. Display Tool Tips

A "Tool Tip" is a beneficial message that appears in Photoshop when your mouse pointer is over a tool or option. Tool Tips are crucial since they provide a brief explanation of what a tool or option is used for, which is very helpful to newcomers who are still trying to find their way around. Tool Tips are by default turned on. They are an excellent method to learn Photoshop if you are new to it. However, if you become familiar with Photoshop, you could feel as though the Tool Tips are beginning to obstruct your work. Simply uncheck "Show Tool Tips" in the Preferences when you no longer feel the need for them.

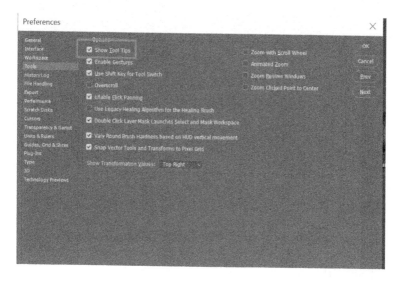

2. Use the Shift Key to Switch Tools

When we use keyboard shortcuts to choose Photoshop's tools, this option has an impact. "Use Shift Key for Tool Switch" is usually turned on.

You will see in Photoshop that similar tools are grouped together to conserve space on the user interface. A fly out menu would appear, for instance, if you clicked on the Lasso tool, letting you know that the Polygonal Lasso Tool and the

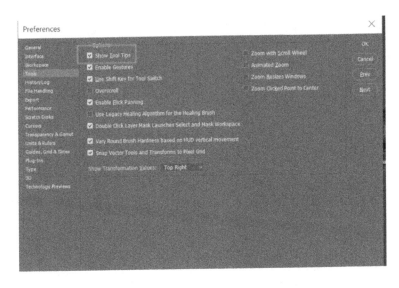

Magnetic Lasso Tool are also grouped together. These gadgets typically share a single keyboard shortcut key.

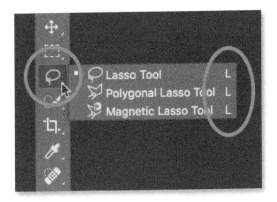

The Lasso Tool will then be selected if you choose to switch tools using the Shift key, which you may do by hitting L on your keyboard. No matter how many times you click L, you can only choose the Lasso Tool; you cannot choose the Polygonal Lasso Tool or the Magnetic Lasso Tool. Holding the Shift Key while pressing L will allow you to choose the Polygonal or Magnetic Lasso tool using the keyboard shortcut. And each tool in the toolbar that uses the same keyboard shortcut follows the same pattern. Simply disable the "Use Shift Key for Tool Switch" option to avoid the potential tension and frustration of this situation. When the option is disabled, you can switch between any tools that have the same keyboard shortcut by simply pressing the corresponding letter.

File Handling Preferences

Among the choices available under File Handling

Preferences are:

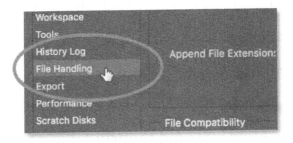

1. Auto Save

The auto save setting instructs Photoshop to periodically save a backup copy of your work. Your work will be backed up automatically every 10 minutes by default. Normally, that is OK. However, you can choose to reduce the interval from 10 minutes to possibly 5 minutes or you can pick the time interval, especially if the backups cause performance concerns, based on how quickly you work and the dependability of your equipment. But keep in mind that extending the backup interval also raises the possibility of losing your work.

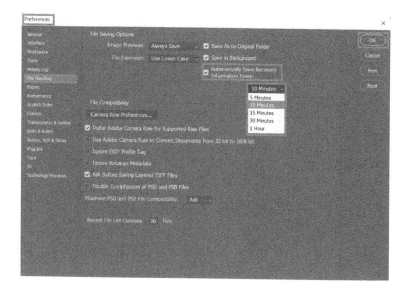

2. Recent File List Contains

The number of files you have previously opened that Photoshop will keep track of is determined by the 'Recent File List Contains' option. Photoshop only records the last 20 projects you have worked on by default, but you may change this to 100 or disable the feature entirely by setting the value to 0.

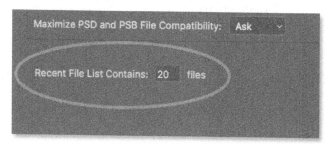

If you do not want others to know what you are working on, you can also set the value to 0.

Performance Preferences

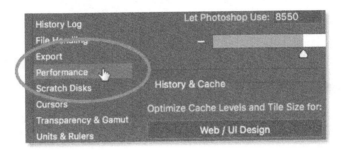

The choices under Performance Preferences include;

1. Use of Memory

The Performance Category's Memory Usage option determines how much of your computer's memory is set aside for Photoshop. The more memory Photoshop has, the more smoothly it tends to operate. By default, Adobe allots Photoshop 70% of your computer's memory. However, you might try raising the RAM usage value if Photoshop continues to have trouble or runs slowly, especially when dealing with large files. You can choose to set the memory consumption to 100%, but keep in mind that other open programs on your device will also use memory. Close all other apps whenever you are using Photoshop as much as you can, but if you must leave one open, lower Photoshop's memory use to 90 or 80%. To make your changes effective, Photoshop must be restarted.

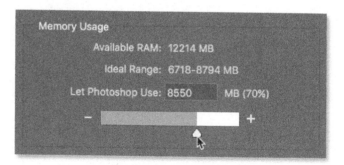

2. History and Cache

The number of steps that Photoshop records as you work is what is meant by the "History States" option. The more steps you can undo to return to a previous state, the more steps it remembers. States from the past are kept in memory. Be aware that too many states can cause Photoshop to run slowly. The default value has been raised all the way to 50 by Adobe. However, unless you absolutely need so many undos, it is advisable that you lower the limit to perhaps 30 or 25. Try reducing the value if you experience performance issues. Once more, in order for the update to take effect, Photoshop must be restarted.

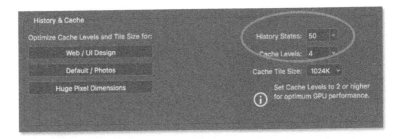

3. Scratch Disks

If your computer's system memory is full, Photoshop can use a portion of the hard drive known as a "scratch disk" as additional memory. Photoshop will not need to use the scratch disk if your computer has enough RAM. Any hard drive(s) you have chosen in the Scratch Disks option will be used if the scratch disk is necessary.

Your computer's primary hard drive is referred to as the startup disk. You might just have this hard disk. If so, it will be chosen by default and you will not actually need to do anything further.

Choose a drive that is not your Startup disk if you have more than two hard drives. Since your operating system makes heavy use of your Startup disk, selecting an alternative drive will improve Photoshop performance. Additionally, if you know the speeds of your hard drives, selecting the fastest disk will improve performance.

4. For Best Performance, Use SSDs

Last but not least, select the SSD (Solid State Drive) as your scratch disk if one of the hard disks on your computer is an SSD. Traditional hard drives are far slower than SSDs, which can significantly increase performance. The best option is still your SSD, even if it also serves as your startup disk. If Photoshop runs out of system memory, it will not ever use your scratch drive. The best results will come from upgrading your computer's memory (RAM) if Photoshop frequently runs out of system memory.

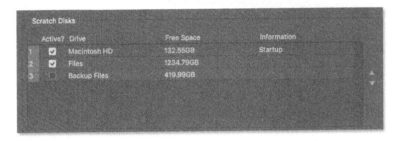

5. The Preferences Dialog Box Is Closed

Click OK to close the Preferences dialog box after accepting your changes. Keep in mind that some of your changes may not take effect until you restart Photoshop.

CHAPTER 5

Photoshop Screen Modes and Interface Tricks

Photoshop users have almost always contended with one frustrating issue, lack of space to properly view their images. The Photoshop interface frequently feels crowded and cluttered since there are so many panels, menus, tools, and options to choose from. And the less space we have for viewing our photographs, the more space the interface takes up. Therefore, it is vital to develop strategies to reduce the interface and increase the work area. While some users have access to two monitors, allowing them to move the panels to one screen while viewing and modifying the image on the other, it is crucial to discover a more workable and affordable option for others.

To tackle this problem, a good understanding and taking proper advantage of Photoshop's screen modes is needed. The amount of the Photoshop interface that is visible on your screen at any given time is controlled by the Screen mode. There are three different Screen mode settings available. Of which they are:

- ▶ The Standard Screen Mode.
- ▶ Full Screen Mode with Menu Bar
- ▶ Full Screen Mode

Location of the Screen Modes

There are two places in Photoshop where you can find screen modes. The first one can be found in the top menu bar. Go up to the View menu in the Menu Bar and pick Screen Mode to access the Screen Modes from there. The Standard Screen Mode, Full

Screen Mode with Menu Bar, and Full Screen Mode can all be selected from this point.

The Screen Modes in Photoshop can be found in two locations. One is located in the screen's top-left menu bar. Select Screen Mode by going to the View menu up in the Menu Bar. You can choose between Full Screen and Standard Screen Mode from this point.

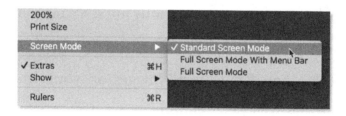

The Toolbar on the left side of the screen is where you can locate the Screen Modes in a second location. You can select a screen mode from a fly-out menu by clicking and holding on the icon for screen mode.

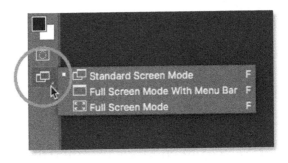

View Modes vs. Screen Modes

View Modes in Photoshop regulate the document's zoom level as opposed to Screen Modes, which reveal or conceal various interface elements. You may choose Fit on Screen from the view menu in the Menu Bar to view images on your screen using one of several methods.

Zoom In	⌘ +
Zoom Out	⌘ −
Fit on Screen	**⌘ O**
Fit Artboard on Screen	
100%	⌘ 1
200%	
Print Size	

Photoshop adjusts the zoom level in the Fit on Screen mode so that the image fills the entire viewable area of the document window. Use the

100% option as another View Mode selection. Simply return to the View menu in the Menu Bar and select 100% this time:

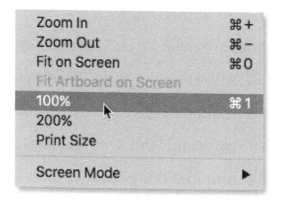

When you switch to 100% View Mode, the zoom level instantaneously increases to 100%, which means that every pixel in the image now occupies exactly one pixel on your screen. The interface is said to be getting in the way at this point because the panels tend to block most of your image from being visible. This view mode would allow you to see your image in full detail, but it would also mean that the image is way too large to fit into the document viewable area. For PCs with smaller screens and lower screen resolutions, this issue is even more problematic.

The Standard Screen Mode

The Standard Screen Mode is applied by Photoshop by default. Here the entire interface ranging from the Panels at the right to the Toolbar at the left is visible. The Menu and Option bars are also visible in this mode, alongside the Status Bar, The Scroll Bar and Tabs. The Standard Screen Mode utilizes the largest screen space, while giving easy access to whatever function we might require.

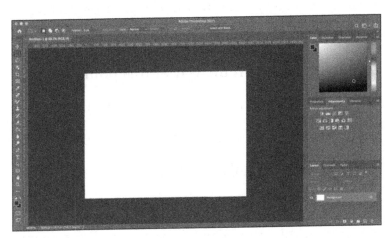

Full Screen Mode with Menu

If you require additional space, you can opt for the Full Screen Mode with Menu Bar. Go to the View menu, click Screen Mode, and then choose Full Screen Mode with Menu Bar for access to this mode. As an alternative, you may choose Full Screen Mode with Menu Bar from a fly-out menu that displays when you click and hold on the Screen Mode symbol at the bottom of the Toolbar.

When utilizing Full Screen Mode with Menu Bar, any interface elements that were a component of the document window itself are hidden. Some UI elements are not visible, but not all of them. The Status Bar, Scroll Bar, and Tab Bar are all affected by this.

Full Screen Mode

You have to switch to the Full Screen Mode if you want to maximize use of your workspace. Go to the View menu, pick Screen Mode, and then click on Full Screen Mode to access this mode. On the other hand, you can select Full Screen Mode from the fly-out menu by hovering over and clicking on the Screen Mode symbol at the bottom of the Toolbar.

Photoshop absolutely masks the UI in Full Screen Mode. The entire screen becomes your work area since just the image stays visible, allowing it complete access to the whole display.

Accessing the Interface from the Sides in Full Screen Mode

While you have succeeded in converting the entire screen into your work area, and have succeeded in eliminating clutters caused by panels, menus, tools and options, you might find it difficult to work when the interface is completely hidden. To have access to the interface without having to switch from one screen mode to the other consistently, you can simply rely on Photoshop's keyboard shortcuts, or learn to do the following:

Activating Full Screen Mode to Display the Toolbar

Simply move your mouse pointer anywhere along the left edge of the screen when in Full Screen Mode to momentarily reveal the Toolbar so you can switch between tools. After choosing a tool, move your mouse cursor away from the edge of the screen, and the toolbar will vanish.

How to leave full-screen mode

When in Full Screen Mode, Photoshop's interface is entirely hidden, therefore you might be wondering how to exit it and restore the interface. You only need to press the Esc key on your keyboard to leave Full Screen Mode. You will then be in the Standard Screen Mode after doing this.

Using the keyboard to reveal and conceal the interface

Directly from your keyboard, you can temporarily reveal and conceal the UI. These keyboard shortcuts are a terrific method to give yourself more space when you need it because they operate in all screen modes, not just full screen mode. Press the Tab key on your keyboard to reveal or conceal the toolbar on the left, the options bar up above, and the panels on the right in any of the three screen modes.

Press Shift+Tab on your keyboard to show and hide only the panels on the right. This function can be employed in all three of Photoshop's screen modes.

How to Change Screen Modes Quickly

The quickest way to changing Screen Modes in Photoshop is still by using the keyboard to cycle through them. You can also access the View menu in the Menu Bar and the Screen Mode icon in the Toolbar. To switch between Standard Screen Mode and Full Screen Mode with Menu Bar, use the letter F on your keyboard. Press F once more to enter full screen mode. You can return from Full Screen Mode to Standard Screen Mode by pressing F one more time. Press Shift+F to go backwards through the screen modes.

CHAPTER 6

Adobe
Firefly

Launched at the Adobe Summit 2023, Adobe Firefly is an exciting new AI software developed by Adobe, the makers of Photoshop that has held the attention of multiple product launches and announcements. Adobe Firefly, though still in its beta stage is already proving to be capable of revolutionizing the creative industry and the field of artificial intelligence (AI). With the simple prompt system in Adobe Firefly, you can enter words or a description, and the program will produce visuals depending on your input. For the time being, only personal usage of the generated photographs is permitted due to Adobe Firefly still being in beta testing. An AI tool called Firefly is getting ready to integrate AI with well-known Adobe programs, enabling users to quickly and easily explore and enhance any concept.

Adobe has entered the generative AI market with the release of Firefly, demonstrating once more that they are at the forefront of innovation in the creative sector. We can anticipate some incredibly strong tools to be published very soon into some of Adobe Firefly's most well-known programs, including Photoshop, Illustrator, Express, and Experience Manager. Although Adobe Firefly's AI models are still in the prototype stage, the demonstrations have been nothing short of amazing. This will provide users access to fresh features including text-to-image conversion, text effects helped by AI, and much more!

Features of Project Firefly

Improvements for Image Enhancing

A few of the truly incredible image editing tools available in Firefly are 3D-to-image conversions, generative fillers, and image extensions. The development of these tools has a significant impact on any designer's creative genius since they allow even a novice designer to produce works of art.

Meta-Content Detecting Images Modeled by AI

This is perhaps one of the most impressive feature of Project Firefly. Images produced with Adobe Firefly have meta-content that says they were produced with AI. This means that the worry for authentic photos is greatly reduced, boosting transparency, credibility and originality in works.

Making Image Enhancement Simple

You may improve pictures and make it easier to transfer styles or compositions of one idea to another by using Adobe Firefly. Your photographs will look more polished and professional thanks to the tool's simple method of adding styles and textures to letters and other objects.

Using Natural Language Processing to Create Images Quickly

Adobe Firefly makes use of natural language processing to produce high-quality visual material that adheres to your specifications by comprehending the intent behind your text description. As a result, you may now produce photos more quickly and effectively than before.

Straightforward navigation and friendly interface

Firefly is extremely easy to use. It has a simple and understandable UI, and this allows even beginners with no prior experience to start using it without encountering difficulties.

Text to Image

Firefly comes with a text-to-image feature. The introduction of this feature means you no longer have to be a professional designer to create dazzling designs; all you have to do us type down your vision in a box and watch it get generated in seconds.

Generative Fill

One of the features that has been added to Photoshop that has been designed to speed up workflow and make working a lot easier is the Generative Fill. With the help of a regular brush and the incredible function known as generative fill, you can effectively delete portions of the background of an image and then render in a completely new background by utilizing simple text prompts. You can use a text prompt and generative AI technologies to generate imagery to fill in blank spaces in an image. It should be emphasized that what makes the Generative Fill function so fantastic is that you can now add more elements, such as new characters, in addition to changing specific backdrop sections. You may change the lighting, as well as the intensity of the shadows.

The new Generative Fill tool achieves beautiful results that would typically need hours or even days to accomplish when edited manually. It does this by matching the "perspective, lighting and style of images," which is what makes it so powerful. Users can add and remove elements from photos using text prompts in addition to Generative Fill. It goes without saying that all of these modifications are done in layers, making it simple to advance and reverse through edits.

What Can Generative Fill Be Utilized for?

You can use any of the given sample images on the Firefly browser to play about and experiment with, or you can upload your own pictures to the Generative Fill tool. Your own photographs will function just as well as the examples given.

You can pick out certain areas of your image that you want to change, tweak, or completely replace using a selection tool. Once you have made your choice, enter a prompt in the text field to indicate what to fill it with. You can easily adjust anything, like changing a character's position from sitting to standing, including another person in the backdrop, and switching from a sunny afternoon to a wet morning. You can navigate through a number of options that are related to your prompt before selecting the one that best fits your needs.

You can modify backdrops, add objects, get rid of defects, extend your image with new, realistic borders, and do a lot more using Generative Fill. The precision of Adobe Firefly's Generative Fill is really high and it seems practically endless.

Gaining Access to Generative Fill

As previously indicated, Firefly is presently in beta. On the project's main page, under the heading "Creating a custom native Adobe Cloud app," you may sign up for a preview.

Adobe will only grant access to organizations, which is unfortunate given that individual developers will need to submit an organization ID. You will be given access after completing a request form.

As previously mentioned, the fact that Adobe guarantees that the created photographs are suitable for commercial usage gives these tools even more strength. Adobe is even adding Content Credentials to works of art, providing users with more information about how the artwork was generated, such as whether it was fully done by hand or if AI provided assistance. As time goes on, Generative Fill will be made generally accessible on the desktop application and Firefly beta.

10 Photoshop Tips for Using Generative Fill to Enhance Your Photos

Without a doubt, the Generative Fill feature has changed the game of editing images. With this powerfully brilliant AI engine, Generative Fill uses Adobe Stock images to lend pixels to our own images for photo editing and creative use. Below are ten ways to use this feature to improve your creative genius

1. Change Expressions and Facial Features

The Generative Fill too has made changing expressions and facial features of characters in images laughably easy. Unlike before where such task was extremely time consuming, you can now change the expression on someone's face with a simple text prompt, like 'smile', 'frown', etc.

To do this correctly, choose more space than you may actually need in order to modify the expression more exactly. This is due to the fact that in addition to the muscles employed to produce the focal area, additional muscles are also used when someone emotes.

2. Increase the Frame Size for Improved Composition

Expanding the frame of your image using the Generative Fill is a nearly valuable function in and of itself. To accomplish this, just enlarge the frame in Photoshop using the Crop Tool, and then use Generative Fill to fill in the blank spaces.

Select Generative Fill, then Generate (leaving the text field empty) to compare the three possibilities. Keep your text brief if you must utilize it to get a different outcome.

In cases like these, it does not matter if the negative space's resolution is low because there are no textural features present; instead, all that is present is color and the attractive shadow that Generative Fill chose to add.

3. Remove unwanted items and individuals

Generative Fill raises the bar for removing undesirable subjects and individuals from a photograph. All you have to do is click while selecting every undesirable pixel. You see what I mean. Click Generate after selecting Generative Fill.

A good general practice is to avoid entering text into the text prompt unless you are not receiving the intended results when you want Generative Fill to simply delete. Otherwise, make the selection(s) using any of Photoshop's selection tools before using Generative Fill and Generate.

4. Alter the color of your outfit

You cannot alter the color of the identical clothing that your subjects are wearing. That is a sophisticated function that most likely will not be available until after Generative Fill exits beta. However, as of this writing, you can alter the color of clothing if you do not mind having part of the actual clothing altered as well. Make sure to limit your choices to only clothing if you want to utilize this feature properly. If you need to make changes to the mask, use the Brush tool.

5. Design people and objects

It is interesting to note that you may add people and objects to your photographs to spice them up. Simply add as many generation frames as you like and enter the necessary information in the text box to accomplish this.

Given the potential resolution challenges, it is worthwhile to consider further options. If Generative Fill does not get the scale quite right for the items or people, use the Transform Tool to make them smaller.

6. Add hats and sunglasses as accessories

It costs almost nothing to bring in extras like hats and sunglasses thanks to Generative Fill. You have to use your imagination. It is quite astonishing that Photoshop manages to capture each object's accurate lighting and reflection in the sunglasses.

Knowing how to use Photoshop's Select and Max workspace can help you make more intricate adjustments.

7. Put a sky in your picture

You may quickly replace the sky in a shot using Photoshop or one of the many other available photo editing programs. However, you can truly add a sky using Generative Fill.

Simply use the Crop Tool to enlarge the frame and Generative Fill to add a sky.

8. Combine more than two images together

You may effortlessly combine two or more photos with the Generative Fill tool. To accomplish this, align the photographs side by side, and then choose. For this, the Rectangular Marquee Tool performs admirably.

9. Build Reflections

Without needing to enter anything in the prompt section, you can construct reflections. This is so that Generative Fill can consider the full image. However, if you want a really great reflection, you might need to crop the image to make more room for it.

Another operation that, in the past, required several stages to do in Photoshop can now be completed with Generative Fill in a matter of seconds.

10. Make an image from nothing

Generative Fill can be used to build images from scratch. Simply select the proportions when you create a New Document in Photoshop. After that, add your choices and build your image frame by frame.

What Photoshop Beta's Generative Fill can produce is quite remarkable. Future updates should provide us more control and greater possibilities.

The Photoshop Landscape Is Changing Thanks to Generative Fill

As previously mentioned, future Photoshop editing and creation will be completely reimagined thanks to AI technologies like Generative Fill. Even though new AI tools will not replace all of Photoshop's features anytime soon, their availability will make it simpler for beginners to learn how to use Photoshop and even become proficient with its user interface without going through arduous and time-consuming training.

Both seasoned Photoshop users and Photoshop beginners should check out what Generative Fill can achieve for their creative processes.

Other Features of Project Firefly

Adobe Firefly is still in beta testing, so as users provide feedback, its tools and features may change. There are currently a ton of fantastic features that will get you started on this new Adobe AI journey.

Text-based Vector Recoloring Prompts

At the time of the announcement, this functionality was not quite ready, but Adobe says it will be out soon. You can produce color changes of vector artwork you have made using a textual prompt.

This method of recoloring visuals is rapid and enables you to explain your ideas for a new color scheme. While recoloring vectors in applications like Illustrator is not very challenging without AI, it will undoubtedly be more accurate and quick with this new tool.

Picture to Text

Adobe has incorporated a text-to-picture tool into Firefly, similar to several other well-liked AI image generators like Midjourney and Stable Diffusion. This is a huge game-changer for the creative imagery business behemoth. You will not need to be a competent designer any longer because you can simply type in the image you have in your head to have it generated in a matter of seconds.

Text-to-image AI creation is popular since it is easy to utilize. This strategy permits a tremendous deal of experimentation and education. Writing a distinct and accurate description yields the best results.

Make textures and text styles for text

This feature styles your text by creating images using a different text-to-image creation style. By drafting a prompt and incorporating it into your writing, you can add textures, styles, and personality to your prose. You can make your text appear as wood, water, a platter of food, a parched desert, or even the sky. There are no restrictions.

What Will Adobe Firefly Look Like in the Future?

Although only Adobe can truly predict what the future holds, it has made some indications about the features that users may look forward to in next Adobe Firefly upgrades.

They include:

a. Inpainting

b. Personalized results

c. 3D to Image

d. Extend image

e. Text to pattern

f. Text to brush

g. Text to vector

h. Sketch to image

i.   Text to template

Inpainting

Any object in an image could be added, removed, or replaced with this capability. You can choose to change the color of a shirt from white to blue using the inpainting option. The replacement image would be created using the instructions from the text prompt, resulting in a number of options from which you could choose based on which best matches your original image.

3D to image

Adobe wants you to use AI to add images or textures to your 3D models so that they can be decorated. Interesting text and typeface production applications can be found in Adobe Firefly. The text effects tools in Adobe Firefly are definitely worth experimenting with because you can easily produce some fantastic results. significant time-savings for

3D designers. Create graphics using the 3D positioning elements that are interactive. Simply select the ideal 3D model and enter relevant keywords.

Text conversion to vector and pattern

Future text-to-vector technology turns your prompt into a complete vector. This and the text-to-image tool that Firefly will introduce are somewhat comparable. This enables you to produce a vector that can be edited in Illustrator as well! The text prompts will maintain patterns. Future versions of Firefly should allow you to generate any kind of graphics that is now possible using Adobe software using text prompts.

What can we anticipate to see?

The goal of Firefly is to give creators the tools they need to:

- ► Try out various design iterations
- ► Easily generate astounding digital experiences

- Add elements to illustrations

- Modify the mood of videos

- Add texture to 3D models

- Remove distractions from images

Video-related AI tool

A preview feature for Premiere Pro also gives us a hint that AI techniques will soon make it simple to change the season or the weather in any scene by simply typing a request into a text box.

This will make videos look even more gorgeous and polished! The timetable, however, is not yet known.

CHAPTER 7

Content
Credentials (Beta)

Adobe Photoshop is working on a feature called
Content Credentials (Beta) that will allow authors
to add information about their provenance to their
exported photos. When activated, Content
Credentials collects information about revisions,
activity, and producer names and ties it to the
image as tamper-evident attribution and history
data (referred to as Content Credentials) when
authors export their finished work.

With the help of this function, information about
the creator of a given work and the resources
employed during the production process can be

shared in an open format. As soon as a producer shares his image with the public, this in turn would give the audience the information they need.

The Content Authenticity Initiative's (CAI) expanding ecosystem of technologies includes Content Credentials (Beta). By developing a standard method to distribute visual content without erasing important contextual information like who created it, when it was developed, and how, Adobe and its 800+ CAI members are committed to reestablishing confidence online. Adobe co-founded the Coalition for Content Provenance and Authenticity (C2PA) with the CAI in order to create a free, universal standard for exchanging this data among platforms and websites.

When Should I utilize Content Credentials (Beta)?

The Content Authenticity Initiative (CAI), a larger endeavor, includes the Content Credentials

(Beta) function in Photoshop. An open, expandable method for recording, modifying, and distributing content with provenance and attribution is the aim of the CAI, an Adobe-led community of creators, technologists, journalists, activists, and educators.

Content Credentials (Beta): When to Use Them

When producers wish to track attribution and add an extra layer of transparency for their audience, the Content Credentials (Beta) function is most helpful. Both amateur and experienced artists can utilize the function to add a layer of trust for the following objectives:

► Attribution to the creator: Creators can utilize Content Credentials (Beta) to record their editing workflow, add revisions, and credit their work in order to share it with their audience. As their contribution is published and distributed, this function also guarantees that they are given credit.

➤ Photographers might record editing information, image history, and attribution to communicate with their audiences in photojournalism.

➤ Non-fungible tokens (NFTs): Before an artwork is added to the blockchain, buyers and sellers of NFTs can view its history and attribution by using Content Credentials (Beta).

Using Photoshop with Content Credentials (Beta)

Activate and accept Content Credentials (Beta)

1. Click the Enable Content Credentials button under Window > Content Credentials (Beta) to enable content credentials for your document. When activated, the panel ought to reload in order to show the attribution

settings. You can also choose Enable Content Credentials from the context menu when you right-click on any open document tab.

2. By heading to Preferences > History & Content Credentials > Content Credentials (Beta) Document Settings, you can additionally make the feature available for all new documents or for documents that already have Content Credentials. In order to ensure that all of your adjustments and activities are recorded and that the history of how your image was created is as precise as possible, we advise selecting Enable for new and saved documents with Content Credentials.

    Keep in mind that Content Credentials (Beta) will only attach content credentials to a picture if the user specifically activates the capability and selects to do so at export time.

3. Select Window > Content Credentials (Beta) to modify your Content Credentials (Beta)

settings. This icon ought to be shown on your panels bar. You can choose what details about your material you want to be associated with it using this panel.

Credentials Preview for Your Work (Beta)

Either pick Preview under Window > Content Credentials (Beta) or click the Content Credentials (Beta) symbol in the panels bar. The following choices will appear:

- **Produced by:** the specified identity of the individual or organization who exported the content.

- **Made with:** the editing program that was utilized to make this work.

- **Edits and activity:** The producer's interventions with the content.

- **Signed by:** the entity claiming ownership of the content credentials.

- **Date signed:** The signer's date of signature on

the document's content.

Credentials for Exporting Work with Attached Content (Beta)

Go to Export As to view your export preferences after your document has been enabled with Content Credentials. You can choose to incorporate Content Credentials with your photographs by selecting Publish to Content Credentials cloud or Attach to file (JPG & PNG) in the Content Credentials (Beta) section. If you select None, your exported picture will not have Content Credentials.

To see how the Content Credentials will seem to others, you can also choose Preview. Export your content as a JPEG or PNG when you are finished. Your final image is ready to use and has the necessary content credentials.

Go to Preferences > History & Content Credentials > Content Credentials (Beta) Export As Options to change the export default settings. To guarantee that your data is always protected, even if it becomes detached from your image, we advise choosing Publish to Content Credentials cloud.

The Content Credentials Cloud

Your attribution and history information is stored publicly and persistently in Adobe's Content Credentials cloud. Your files will stay smaller by publishing to this cloud, and your Content Credentials will be more durable. The cloud-stored Content Credentials can be found through a search if your image's Content Credentials are ever removed.

Users can choose this in Preferences or the Export dialog if they desire to store their Content Credentials in the file.

View on Verify Your Content Credentials

To check your Content Credentials on the online Verify viewer, select your image. This viewer may be used to verify any image's content credentials, view a list of the components used to create the image, and compare versions to observe how the image has changed over time.

Supported File Types

During this beta, Content Credentials (Beta) only supports exporting JPG and PNG files.

Are the released materials missing your content credentials?

When an image is loaded or published, many digital programs and utilities remove image metadata, including data pertaining to Content Credentials (Beta). When you upload an image online and discover that the content credentials are missing, it is probably because the application does not yet support Content Credentials (Beta).

You can reconnect the content credentials on Verify if you exported your image using the Content Credentials cloud.

System requirements for Content Credentials (Beta)

- Internet access

- Creative Cloud or Photoshop subscription

- Intel/ARM processors on Macs and Windows computers

- Mac OS 10.15.7 or later

- Windows 10 (64-bit) version 1809 or later

- Operating systems

- Intel/ARM processors

- Operating systems

- Browsers

- The two most recent versions of these browsers for Mac & PC are: Chrome and Firefox, which depend on the operating system of your device, are only available on Macs, while Microsoft Edge is only available on Pcs.

- Administrators of systems: These endpoints, cai.adobe.io and cai-identity.adobe.io, must be accessible by the system.

CHAPTER 8

20 Photoshop Tricks and Techniques That All User Should Know

Try the following tips to get a great experience out of Adobe Photoshop and unlock your creative genius.

1. Pick out your colors from any location.

Instead of taking a screenshot of something in order to capture its colors, just use the Eye Dropper tool, dismiss Photoshop, click the dropper onto your canvas, and then drag it wherever you need it outside of Photoshop.

2. Photoshop's Warp Text function

Look to the top-right of the Type Tool's toolbar while the Type Tool is chosen, active, and on your text layer. A "T" icon with a curved line underneath will be seen. Press that icon to view a variety of pre-built text arcs and bends.

3. Download creative Photoshop brushes

Install one of the tens of thousands of brush possibilities available online instead of feeling constrained by the Photoshop brushes that come pre-installed. In order to accomplish this, select Import Brushes from the Gear icon.

4. Make an instant light bleed effect

To accomplish this, make a new layer and use a large, fluffy white brush to paint white toward the top of your image. This will add a faint light bleed to help merge any image. Reduce the layer's opacity to wrap up it.

5. Layer Styles to Copy Quickly

Drag the FX symbol from the original layer to the desired layers while holding down the Alt key. The layer styles will be promptly applied.

6. Create various text stroke effects

To apply the Stroke layer effect, double-click the text layer. To add an additional Stroke, click the Plus symbol. Feel free to include as many as you like!

7. Combining Forms

By choosing your shape layers and selecting Right-Click > Merge Shapes, you can quickly build custom shapes utilizing the shapes you have already made. This would combine all of your different shapes into one.

8. Using Motion Blur

Create a feathered selection around an object's edges and then add a modest Filter > Blur > Motion Blur to give any object a sense of motion.

9. Sort Through Your Brushes

The days of disorganized, chaotic brushes are long gone! To organize and arrange your brushes, go to the Brush panel and select Right-Click > Create Group.

10. Utilize Photoshop's Refine Edge tool

You need to extract everything manually, however the Quick Selection tool is not working for you. Make a fast selection of the area surrounding your subject, then double-click the Layer Mask you just added. Decide on Select and Mask. The Refine Edge Brush may be found right here. After checking the Smart Radius box, start brushing. The edge will be nearly flawlessly refined using Photoshop!

11. Add a Layer for Color Lookup

Want to give your photograph a quick color grade? Utilize the less well-known Color Lookup adjustment layers in Photoshop! They are a fantastic place to start for any color grade because there are so many presets to pick from.

12. Photoshop guides can be made

In Photoshop, you can make a guide by simply clicking and dragging on the side rulers. By pressing Control-R, you can bring in the rulers if you cannot see them.

13. Photoshop: How to Get Rid of Color Banding

Do you have issues with color banding? Make a new layer, fill it with black, add a light Noise filter, and then set the layer to screen to get rid of that banding. This will lessen banding and aid in spreading the colors.

14. Ink and makeup

Make a new layer, change the blend mode to Soft Light, then add the eyeshadow by hand! You can unleash your creative brilliance by using the Soft Light and Overlayer layer modes, which will make you an expert post-production makeup artist.

15. Change the brush size and hardness quickly

Did you know that you may modify the size of your brush by using the square bracket keys [and]? To alter the brush's hardness, you can alternatively press the bracket keys while pressing Shift. All of this is done without using the Brush panel!

16. Change the Flow Rate of a Brush

Lower the brush's Flow after selecting the brush and looking up at the top toolbar. Now, every stroke of the brush will gradually add color, making it ideal for lighting and shadowing.

17. Remove Layers Quickly

When you want to concentrate on one layer, the others get in the way. Click on the Eyeball icon for the layer you want to isolate while holding down the Alt key. Alt-clicking again will turn on the additional levels immediately.

18. Pressure-sensitivity is activated

Do all brushes on a tablet support pressure sensitivity? Enter the Brush Settings, Shape Dynamics, and set Control to Pen Pressure and Minimum Diameter to 0% to activate it.

19. Enjoy using Photoshop filters

Photoshop filters, as you may have guessed, are essentially automated effects that you can apply to your photographs with a few clicks to generate specific special effects or looks. Although they are simple to operate, they produce excellent results.

20. Sharpen up for more impact

The sharpness of most photographs can be slightly increased to improve detail, emphasize texture, and give your files a little more punch.

But how might Photoshop image sharpness be enhanced?

To make things as simple as possible, choose Filter>Sharpen>Unsharp Mask. You may then

choose a sharpening Amount in the dialog; larger numbers enhance the sharpness effect.

Made in the USA
Monee, IL
28 August 2023

41742924R00075